EMPOWERMENT:
INSIDE
OUT

EMPOWERMENT: INSIDE OUT

TRENITA WALKER

Library of Congress Control Number:		2020910505
ISBN:	Hardcover	978-1-9845-8293-5
	Softcover	978-1-9845-8292-8
	eBook	978-1-9845-8291-1

Print information available on the last page.

Rev. date: 07/20/2020

To order additional copies of this book, contact:
Xlibris
1-888-795-4274
www.Xlibris.com
Orders@Xlibris.com
809492

Contents

Testimony

PSALM 51:10

'Create in me a clean heart, O God, and renew a right spirit within me.'

Often times we as individuals ask for the lord to remove a mountain that we may face daily on the job in our relationships with different people. Or occasionally such as finances or health situations. And that is fine, but as a Christian believer what if it is not the mountain that needs to be moved? What if it is the way we see the mountain that needs to be moved. Amen. Our outlook and perspective on situations can determine how a situation will turnout. Job is a righteous man...and in the book of job in the Old Testament chapter 1 v.s 6-12.

The lord presents job to Satan and Satan goes and set forth many tribulations in job's life. (job1:13-22) Now in the midst of losing family and property job simply replied "naked came I out of my mother's womb, and naked shall I return: the lord gave, and the lord hath taken away; blessed be the name of the lord." what a humble spirit to have in the presence of God in the midst of calamity!!l instead of move the mountain from his life, job simply acknowledge the lord as the giver and provider and the creator that can do what he wants and when he wants. Amen. And further on into the story job was wealthier than he was before the trials came to him. God blessed him double for enduring everything. No matter what we face let us not focus on the mountain we see in front of us but focus on the king above us by simply acknowledging him. And pray for the power to overcome the mountain through the lords will and way not ours. Amen.

John 1:9: Ill we confess our sins, he is faithful and just to forgive us our sins, and to cleanse us from all unrighteousness. Often times we want to move forward but cannot because of past sins that we committed within our lives. Amen. But our father within heaven lets us all know that if we talk to God and confess our wrong doings through prayer he will forgive us and we can be freed within our minds and souls. Amen. God will take the pain away and lift the weight of the past away!!!

It is all in me:

Queen Iam
Meant to be
Is all in me.

The King Iam meant
To be is all
In me.

The riches
Is the gold
That pours out
Of my soul.

The rubies
Is the crystal
That shines
As I turn into
The diamond.

No more why?
More
Yes..

To your will
Yes to your way!!!

Spiritual freedom
Mental peace
Talking but quite!!
All negative cease!!

Cease fire
Time to go higher
No more war
Time to channel
The inner star
To quit can't
Come to far!!!

I am powerful
I am strength
I am happiness
I am everything
Let the earth sing!!
Mountain high

Valley low
Wherever the Lord
Leads I will go!!

I am Humble
Not boastful
I am successful
Not stressful

I am grateful
Not hateful

I am victorious
Not a victim
I am wealthy
Not getting by
I hold my head up high
Not walking down low!!!
I walk beside my half
not behind my half
I am intelligent
not ignorant

I am open minded
Not closed minded
I am blessed
Not depressed!!
Ego: Eternal growth onward
GOD's child!!!

I Am:

I am

Someone

I am

Unique

I am

Shinning

I am

Soft

I am

Strong

I am

Different

I am

Out spoken

I am me!!!

Loving everything about

Me...

I am me!!

Not this time:

Not this time
No
Not this time
Got me once
Got mc twice
My heart
You took apart and sliced!!!
No
not this
Time!!!
Lied, covered up,
Lied cover up,
Lied, hide
Held everything
On the inside.
My soul died.
No
Not this time,
No
Not this time!!
What I tripped on
I walked over
What I slipped on
I skipped over.
Not this time
No not this time...
This time is
My time!!!

God already

Know about it!!

"Come unto me...!

Come all

Come all

Ye shall know the truth..!!

And you shall be free!!!

The world says

Unforgiven

God says

Forgiven!!

The world says

Hate no love

God says

The greatest of these three is love.'

I love you!!!

What God says

The world say

Ugly

Beautiful

The world misunderstands

God guides your

Hand

And walks by

You in the

Beautiful sand.

Welcome to his land

Don't be afraid

To hold his hand

Cry about it

Talk about it

Shout about it

Make no doubt

About it

It's okay

It is okay

To be okay

It is okay to

Go from victim

To victorious

It is okay

To forgive

Those that "hurt' you

It is okay

To live

It is okay

To smile

It is okay

To be happy

It is okay

To be okay

Unbury the hurt

On this day

Because you are

Okay!!

Weeping may endure for the moment

Joy comes in the morning..'

It's okay!!

Within Me!!

It is love
It is joy
It ls peace
It ls deep
It ls down ln my soul
Within me!!!
It is unity
It is freedom
It is deliverance
It is inspiration
It is deep
It ls down within my soul
Within me!
It is God within me

Jesus Saves

No matter how low
No matter how bad
No matter how hurt
Jesus saves!!!
You might be experiencing difficulties
You might be experiencing pain
You might be experiencing grief
No matter how much you are experiencing
Jesus saves!!!
Jesus saves
The low
The weary
The weak
The depressed
The sinners
You have a friend
Jesus saves
Restores
Rebuild
And heals
And open up doors to his will.
Joy
Love
Peace
Trust
In the name of Jesus.
Jesus Jesus Jesus
Is his glorious name
Always staying the same!
Jesus saves!!! Selah!!

Preparing me

Each day
Each hour
Each minute
The Lord say
"I will have my way
A peace of mind
As he walks
And travels
With and for me
Through lifetime.
No dead ends
No uturns
No red lights
Just the lord
And I together
Conversing all
Through the night!
Guiding my feet
Protecting my soul!
Taking my hand
To my next goal!!..Amen!
#No weapon formed against me shall prosper.,
I speak it
I believe it
I receive it!!
Preparing me
Loving me
Guiding me
Keeping me

And most of all
Blessing me!!l
For the whole world to see
..Thou prepares a table in the
Presence of my enemies...
Preparing me!

You

You are loved
You are someone
You matter
You must climb
Your ladder!
Your mountain top
Awaits
No matter how high
Or high low
Your mistake
It's your time!!
You can win
You can win
Again you can win it
Over and over again
The Lord forgives
You can win!
In Christ you have a friend!

I am me!!!

I am me
And I am
Loving me..
Not half of me
Not some of me
Yes all of me!
My past forgiven
My present is holding me
My future is growing me
I cannot wait to see me
I am loving me
And I am me!!!

Change!!!

Change is good
Look deep within
And it is with patience
And understanding
Change is for
The betterment
For the empowerment
No more low self esteem
No more being broken
No more being damaged
Time to be the seed
Planted in good soil
Growing In Iove and peace!!!
Change from the old
To the new
Letting go of the
Old you
And growing into the new you...
Hello me
Goodbye old you
Bye to the
Abuse
Bye to the loneness
Both is of
No use
The past teaches you
The present guards you
And thy future
awaits you!!!
You are somebody
Be proud be bold!!!

Breaking out
From the old
Transforming into Gold!!!
Let your soul shine
And your heart stay kind
You are someone important
Dreams, goals, reality!!!
Change, Arrange,
Rearrange,
From the caterpillar
To the butterfly
You too
Can and will fly!!!
Change

Behind me!!!

My past
Is behind
My present
Is holding me
My future
Is controlling
me.
All the hurt
Was for me
Too see
The king and queen
Within me
The shame
The guilt
Is behind
Me
The praise
The thanks giving
I am that I am..
I am not who I was
I am being who I am
Am becoming who I am
Within me!!
All past mistakes
Behind me!
Broken dream
Behind me all hurt and plan
Behind me
The lord made every thing disappear
behind me in the past
In front of me

I have nothing
But love to gain...
Behind me
besides me
Next to me
All around me!
Gods love surround me
Behind me
No longer bounding me
I am free!!!
Behind me!!

I am here

When you are hurting
I am here
When you are hopeless
I am here
When you are faithless
I am here
When you are weak
I am here
When you are tired
I am here
When you are lost
I am here
When you are grieving
I am here
When you are wondering why I am here.
Will never leave you nor forsake you.
I am here always!!!
Love GOD!!

Love waits

Love waits
Love don't
Rush
Love ls seen
Love ls
Not hush.
Your body
ls your temple
You are beautiful
Just that simple.
Love ls
Passionate
Love ls forever
Love is not
Past tense!!!
Love understands
You.
Love puts your
Feelings first
love lifts you.
When you are at your worst
love lifts you.
Love Is the light
Love ls life
Not lust or a passionate
Night
Love!!!

Upgrade U!!!

When your down
I will be your hope
And come around
And be your peaceful sound.
Let me
Mold you
Let me
Hold you
Let me
Upgrade u!!
Diamonds,
Rubies
Street paid with Gold
Let me
Take care
Of the haters with
Love!!
I will be your
Motivator...
Let me upgrade your soul!!
Let me be the general in
Your army!
Who fights all your
Battles!!!
The race is not
Given to the swift.
Let me uplift
And shift you!!!
Time for that new new.
Blessings after blessings
Get the picture you seeing heaven

Take my hand
With me you can stand
To loosing
Never again
Becoming a new woman and new man!!!
Upgrade you!!!
Victim to Victorious
Once was hurt
Now healed
Once was wounded
Now healed
Once was broken
Now put together
Once was angry
Now have joy.
Once was burden
Now I am bold
No more
Feeling sorry!
No more carrying
A load!!
No more victim
I am victorious

Healed

When I cry
I am healing
When hurt
I am healing
When I am feeling
Emotional
I am healing
When I open up
I am healing
When I accept life at all stages
I am healing., amen
When I forgive I am healing
When I live
I am healed
By his stripes I am healed.
Healed

Lightning Source UK Ltd.
Milton Keynes UK
UKHW011839300720
367452UK00002B/53/J